T0147051

SLANKY

poems

MIKE DOUGHTY

Soft Skull Press • New York

Slanky
Copyright © 1996 by Mike Doughty
This edition published 2012

All rights reserved under International and Pan-American Copyright Conventions. No part of this book may be used or reproduced in any manner whatsoever without written permission from the publisher, except in the case of brief quotations embodied in critical articles and reviews.

This book is a work of fiction. Names, characters, places, an incidents either are products of the author's imagination or are used fictitiously. Any resemblance to actual events or locales or persons, living or dead, is entirely coincidental.

For more information on Mike Doughty visit
www.mikedoughty.com

Library of Congress Cataloging-in Publication is available.
ISBN 978-1-59376-504-0

Cover design by Benjamen Purvis, Gerilyn Attebery
Interior design by Neuwirth & Associates, Inc.

Soft Skull Press
New York, NY
www.softskull.com

Printed in the United States of America

I'll Be Your Babydoll, I'll Be Your Seven-Day Fool

Tonight the train is a curveball

sloping towards portions of

Darkest Brooklyn; some house unlit,

like a blank face, where I assume

you sit unsatisfied in a cubical room.

In the Mind of the Mind

His mind is an angry place. When he is drunk, and can't explain himself, he says his mind is broken. Then he smacks his head repeatedly with the ball of his hand. Everybody laughs.

His mind is something that is very angry with him.

His mind is an angry sea of colors and references. His body bobs alone in it. His mind is an America for jingles and mottoes. Proud detergent names and happy cartoon animals with bow ties. They flock to him on ships. They labor on the assembly lines, screwing and drilling on the components of his dreams. They come out in the morning, smudged with soot.

His dreams are complex and ridiculous, Hong Kong epics of bullets and swords. Flying punches. Homely women in princess drag. Their reaching arms are draped with jewels. He slays her enemies but never screws her. His mind is indifferent to fucking. Though he pleads with it. A white arm emerges from behind the door and hangs a Do Not Disturb sign on the gilded knob. Every time. Then the credits roll, and his mind bills itself as best boy, electrician, cinematographer, gaffer, technician, Man In Hotel Lobby Number Two. Every time. Every time.

His mind is a jealous mind, always campaigning for his attention with garish colors and melodies. Waving its hands in front of his face to obscure the exterior influences. Even as those influences are welcomed inside and incorporated into the process of seduction.

And those influences that refuse the invitation become the object of murderous thoughts. Because the mind has only thoughts for hands, a murderous thought is in the mind the equal of murder. And the job becomes selling the pitch to its corporeal accomplice. But the sin is done.

Because the mind hates what is too big to swallow.

For Charlotte, Unlisted

Her room is still; a bed, a desk, and the one word Easy on

typing paper taped to the wall. This is eight years later, still

dreaming that room this night, alone, the hand drifting

down—a gasp is gasped but the room still sits around me in

its own July; the air there like walking underwater or through

olive oil in a pan; the sheets quick to the skin like icing, her

wide hips forcing my skinniness against the wall.

I fall to the carpet and drift off, the soul travelling to a

nightclub behind a door deep in Sleeptown, and it's her, eight

years later, same eyes and hands and everything, taking tickets.

The hour? I ask. How much? She gives the same answer as last

time: No. There. No. More to the left. The back. Anywhere.

Again. Please.

Rootless

We roamed across Texas in a rented car,

buzzing with aimlessness, squinting

in the dull, hard light.

The greenery shooting past us slowly hardened,

turning into desert, burning away like a menthol into space.

We stopped on a gravel flatland

to piss and smoke, wandering off

to the powerlines at the edges

of our eyes' grasp. Onward.

By the junction, up on the panhandle,

you slept, mumbling a pulp of words

to an unseen companion.

The air curling out of your nose,

droning into your mouth

like a kiss reversed on itself.

Your eyes flashed open and threw down

a bleary glance at the white dashes

and shut again. I could smell you.

My head bent, straining through the whoosh,

to listen. The baby words fell from your lips,

and I sifted them for music,

trying to hear the meaning

in a sucking sound.

Other Fish

A girl with a backpack on a cellular phone sighs;

between the exhale and the first consonant

a van barrels through her. And who knows

what the boy thinks, his line slipping from her voice,

her words sucked backwards through the wire?

Two hours from now he'll be drunk,

his slurred thoughts slobbering over motives,

why she decided suddenly to leave him

and hung up mid-word.

The phone yelps angrily from under a bus,

and she lays splayed like an asterisk

in the dreary sentence of Fourteenth Street.

From a Gas Station Outside Providence

This kiss, unfinished,

lips to receiver in the parking lot,

a pucker shot through a fiber optic wire

to an answering machine

toward switchboards and stations transmitting

in blips to satellites, this kiss

thrown earthward and shooting down

coils, around pipeline and electric power

lumbering underground,

up threads and transistors

and transference points.

This kiss is zeroes and ones jumbled

and tossed into a pneumatic system,

unscrambled at the end and scrawled

onto a tape recorder slowly rolling

at the side of your bed,

then slapping back, reverbed

off the ringer, a tinny phantom

of the smooch like a smack on

an aluminum can, up the same

veins through the belly of the same satellite

and softly to the side of my head;

this kiss is home before the next exhalation leaves.

I'm stooped in the booth,

pounding quarters into the slot;

yellow light droops over the asphalt,

and your ghost, too cool

and elusive with those hands and mouth

sings around me in the smell of gasoline;

whose mouth is this, scratched in static,

some droplet of a sigh, atomized,

and sputtering digitized into my room?

Nerve Injections

A man has premonitions of his teeth cracking every time he looks at concrete. Like the converse of an amputee's ghost pain, he can't feel it but his mouth acts as if he can. He feels his teeth as one solid plate, his mouth dammed with china. He becomes so sick of his teeth screaming that he goes to an unlicensed dentist in a seedy quarter and is injected in his mouth with painkillers to numb them. He becomes an addict but denies this to himself and walks around pillowed from the world.

Later, he freefalls on ice. He carries his teeth home in his wallet. He reassembles the cracked ones with tile epoxy on the kitchen table. He puts them in the icetray in his freezer. For the rest of his life a slathering junkie, he gums hard candy unaware that splinters of jawbreaker are slitting gashes in the sockets in his jaw.

Sound Against the Equal Sign

Behind wire frames, a mind narrows like a splinter of light

through a magnifying glass and onto a withering ant. All

arithmetic predicates itself on a notion of balance; wild

growths of equations differ like species of birds, but even that

disharmony is made similar as taxpayers by the equal sign.

Those parallel lines; a thin mouth, expressionless. He's easy

with the split of his worlds; the illogic that runs through the

brains of people he buys milk from is shadowed by a world

in which a shape will transpose itself, with a shrug, into a

hypotenuse.

In a clarinet, there is no sense. In a swell of brass, there is

no balance. Music is the weird cousin of math; the symbols

grow unchecked, without an equational mirror to justify

them. No other desire is so maddening; to drool over a pear

placed seductively on a table manifests a physiological need.

To let his eyes wander to a pair of thighs manifests a genetic

imperative. Sound is the perception of a wave created by the

movement of object against object against air. Harmony is

the manifestation of a tone above another tone. Hearing a confection of violins, he shakes off his pleasure angrily; all numbers have names and surnames of exponentials and zeroes, but the notes lurk everywhere as faces with nothing but eyes.

His mind defeats itself in attempting to quantify this; all sound carries a logical tonality, he thinks, and trains himself to notice this. The clack of a heel on a staircase produces a matter-of-fact D sharp. Carhorns harmonize with dialtones in a droning G. The notes of all things waver not only on the absolute tones, but on a million points between them, dividing and subdividing in a random, infinite slash into the flesh of the mathematical world.

Sitting sullenly at his desk, spinning a pencil, he suddenly hears a doorbell collide with a cough over the subsonic hum of a television, and leaps up with joy. His face drops. He is lost.

Portraits in Show Business
Number One

On the street they come up to Fran Tarkenton and tell
him about their disappointments, their failures, their dead
marriages. They want a brass cure, accomplished and shiny
like a Heisman trophy. They tell him, Fran Tarkenton, we're
hurting, you're an award-winning broadcaster and former
All-American, come back to our life and save us. But Fran
Tarkenton cannot help them, and he goes to sleep in hotel
rooms on his lecture tours and is troubled by the hell of the
lives of the people.

Fran Tarkenton goes to the President, who is his friend, and
tells him that the marriages of the people have died. The
President goes to the television station and tells knock-knock
jokes on the air. He tells them to get together and love one
another. The people, who elected him, are soothed.

The FBI has Fran Tarkenton killed, on television, and blames
it on the President and a man who they happened to employ
as a bicycle messenger nine years ago, and who happened to

have a shotgun on him that day when he went to his job at
the television station. Because he was going to shoot his wife.
The FBI does not want the people to get together and love
one another.

Portraits in Show Business
Number Two

Joe Franklin was known to ply his guests with bottled water,
extravagant because he bought it and it tastes like nothing.
He wore an indigo dress. The lovable Marky Mark was there.
His drummer was in the midst of a painful divorce, and the
cameraman fell down repeatedly but always got up in time.
They sang "Mr. Funny Man." Seven angels slew the beast Joe
Franklin sat upon behind the desk and cut off his arms, which
had become snakes and spat poison spit on Victor Borge.
Victor Borge, who had found Jesus that afternoon on an exit
ramp, instantly vanished and was in heaven.

Portraits in Show Business
Number Three

Cookie Monster, burnt out and hateful of children, concocts
a suicide plot under the auspices of televised entertainment;
stripped and chained up, he is lifted into a velvet sack, placed
in a steamer trunk full of holes so as to sink faster, sealed, and
thrown into a lake before throngs. The band plays, and in
the sealed trunk, in the velvet sack, Cookie Monster waits to
drown.

When I Was Small

When I was small, when I was very small, I would lay by the television and dream of the apocalypse. I would dream of the power of the Hydrogen Bomb. I dreamed my world engulfed in a divine and furious fire. I hoped for it.

When I Saw It

It was in the garden. I went there, and I looked. And when I saw it, I could not help but to desire it.

I had to pull back the branches to see it. It was late, and the forms of the branches were cast dark against the dark blue sky. There was light, but it huddled to the side of the house. The light flickered over it, randomly, in moments, peekabooing its mysteries. I pulled back the branches, and I looked.

Its sound was like breathing sounds underwater. I could barely hear the sound. And there was a hissing in the air. So I had to strain. I had to tilt my head and push my ear to it.

After this, I would always strain to listen. It was meaningless to look. I met a woman once and told her about this. But she would get angry when I didn't look at her when I spoke. When she spoke, I would push my ear toward her, and she would grab my chin and pull my face to face her. She would think I wasn't listening when I wasn't looking. I left her, but sneakily, just quietly withdrawing myself from her life. She is still angry about that.

She made an amazing sound. I don't know how she made it. I don't remember what the sound sounded like, but I remember the way it filled me. And she had a smell that my mind convinced me was not perfume, but her. I don't remember what the smell smelled like, but I remember the way it filled me. Unlike the sound, though, I am reminded of it when that perfume passes by on other women.

I thought she was the answer. She was not the answer. I have continued to look for the answer, but I have not found it. Instead, I have gained an astounding skill in locating flaws. The answer was simple once, the way math looks in childhood, two digits and a symbol. The answer is a beast now, with tangents and greek numerals, cubed and multiplied. Its algebra has grown unchecked.

It was in the garden. I went there, and I looked. And when I saw it, I could not help myself but to desire it.

❖　❖　❖

I could tell you about the first time I kissed her, which was so compelling it shot me with fright. I could tell you about the first time I saw the way the bone of her hip curves from the side. Lust is ugly like this, this kind of lust where you keep making phonecalls and phonecalls, anxious to see if her voice still exists. Where she becomes mildly creeped when you stare while she reads her book. And she lashes back with vengeful amorousness, such that the sex ceases to be sex, and becomes a brawl of each prying the other open.

Thousands of months have passed since that time. She continues to call me. She says I am unlike anyone else she has ever slept with, in that she continues to call me. She told me about them all. She told me about the one that got her pregnant, and how after that whatever was between them died, and how she believes that as a species in context we are here to yield replacements, and that when this fails, the mind starts chasing other options, elsewhere. She told me about the woman she slept with, who was a minor friend in school. For weeks after she was saddened by the subtle incongruities between those who mostly love those who are like them and those who mostly love those who are unlike them. She told me about the boy she fucked on a boat in the Gulf of Mexico.

She has their phone numbers on scraps in a desk drawer. I've see them spilling out when she opens it.

So when she called me, I went back there, to her house. And when I got there, she was on the phone. But her hand moved across me while she talked on the phone. And she hung up the phone, and we stumbled backwards, upstairs, kissing, up to the bed. And were all but fucking before we fell on to it.

It was in the garden. I went there, and I looked. And when I saw it, I could not help myself but to desire it.

My Lover Lives on the Other Coast

I do what

my baby bids

me do;

across this side-effect of manifest destiny

I fly

to you.

All This from Two Eyes Twitching

Some sallow accountant of dreams

has spilt pop on the margin

of the ledger of your memory,

blurred the ink itemizing

this object and that individual

now starring as Loss or Indecision

in tonight's cinematic rendering

of current events.

Now the whole business is ruined

with sweetness and blended irreparably;

the landscape is caked with sugar,

the plot is a saccharine mess,

and as you fuck some neutral hybrid

of your mother and a boy from the sixth grade,

your mouth purses from a sickly honey taste.

Your nightmares have gone to cheery filmic convention.

When the alarm clock invades,

it's a blast from the trumpets

of the heroes, on white horses,

returned to slay the monster chasing you.

Insomnia

My love and my sleep

light their smokes off

the kitchen stove,

sucking at the blue fire

on the grill.

They stare each other down

with dull eyes

kissing glances

eye tag

look-and-lookaway

while

through the next room's wall

my body sprawls

like a colossus prone

on a bed and blankets landscape

I'm hearing shuffling,

pace, return, shuffling,

fingers drumming

on the counter, a tattoo

drumming up soldiers

to formation.

When morning slips the bolt

off the lock and slides

into the living room easy

I will empty the ashtrays

and receive the fruit of

their negotiations

then sleep the day dry

with their alignment pact

on the bedside table.

This is my song in lieu of dreams,

four a.m., no matches, no coffee, quarter moon.

Peter Mack

They hooked some massive weight

to the underside of his jaw

and left it there for his formative years,

stretching it cartoonish, grim,

and disquietingly long, and left him,

fluvial in his suit and tie

to wade through the world

with a frown concave in that

astounding chin, muttering

in singsong: Whaaaaat?

A Miami for the Talk Show Hosts

They built a city out of raw stucco in the swamps by the ocean for the talk show hosts to go die in. Creaking, still in the blue suits from wardrobe that they wore to entertain America from cue cards. Now, playing chess at their very own desks with special imaginary guests and broken microphones installed by the management as a concession to their paranoid demands, they all talk like mad sportswriters and go all fuzzy in the subtropical heat, looking back bitterly on careers as sleeping aids. They've all gone to conspiracy theories that grew on them like a mold, they all check their meals in the cafeteria for poison and are alert for the ruses of the dreaded network police.

A barren, violent place, there have been stabbings over arguments of who knew Liza best. "Is this aberration how we reward those who have served their country well?" one was heard asking moments before another lunged at him with a pencil. "Look in my wallet, here, these are my grandchildren and my demographics; a couple more points I woulda been in Malibu with Dick Van Dyke, not here festering with a mutt like you."

Jungle of Numbers
a deck of cards

1.

In the mind of my mind,

a hand solders

motives to coils.

2.

He embraced his lawyer.

3.

Geography pulls no magic on me,

today.

4.

In transit, pursued

by his managers.

5.

Over like it never was and

exhausted like a dead man

he looked down and knew

the red in her mouth.

6.

Who was the Egypt's Pharaoh of

the Honkytonk Blues?

7.

Shoulders pushed back,

it leans toward the daylight

and into the eye of noon.

8.

The Sultan

9.

The Magnate

10.

The Inscrutable Deejay McMonkey

11.

The Prime Dog

12.

Everybody needs a hook;

my hook is the fez.

13.

Here comes the Bliss Boy

14.

Swank

15.

Lies

16.

The Hand of the Unknown

17.

The Hand of Unseen Sequence

18.

The Hand of Randomness

19.

The Hand of Unspeakable

Languages

20.

The Calculating Engine

21.

You're the kind of girl that would

break up Van Halen

22.

Herbal Mama?

Herbal Mama.

23.

Elliot Groffman, attorney-at-law,

riding elephants

in the mountains

of Thailand.

24.

He counted in his head,

drifting, as the radiator cooed.

25.

I hope you get there.

I hope you enjoy yourself.

26.

Cruel and unusual.

27.

As the band laughed,

her finger traced his spine,

and he folded into her.

28.

B is for bird, who bit a boy and

tore his eyes out. For breaking all

his toys.

29.

The spiny creatures of the deep

30.

Under your pillow, the gun

breathes.

31.

Shackled with contractual

obligations.

32.

Superstars of the Hong Kong

Cinema!

33.

No toy duck, firetruck!

34.

Pulling gears

to hear the switches click;

feeling a gust of nerves.

35.

An organ chord,

chintzy, rippling,

wavering towards Venus.

36.

Randall Davis Kaye

could not dance

to any kind

of music.

37.

All is Lost

38.

The runt of all numbers;

the number of all runts

39.

Milk and Cigarettes

40.

Sin Will Find You Out

41.

In the lobby,

thousands

of regal women from

accounting,

their hair in smart slants,

heels stinging the floor

like a rain of cutlery

drumming on the Parthenon

42.

All hopped up on goofballs

43.

Far off,

above the Flatbush Extension,

a plane scraped its belly

across a sooty yellow moon.

44.

She found her bliss between the

headphones, and pursed her lips.

45.

Do you have any dolls that can

walk or talk?

46.

Her white neck. By the open door.

47.

She had a long nose, and curves as
sharp as the letter 'X'.

48.

He watched the bodies, fluid in the
lagoon.

49.

Shoveling coal into the open grate.

50.

Driving under a tangle of overpasses.

51.

She watches the record spin,
pained by surfacing dreams
of bourbon and cigarettes

52.

I'll saw those suckers down.

53.

But sleep won't come.

54.

Texas vs. France, who wins?

Here Comes the Panic Now

What do the dogs know?

On Camrose, in a jumble of lots,

the barking came through stucco

with flowers cut into the wall.

What tremor comes, unheard,

gathering its roll now in the hills,

to rush in and sway the palm trees,

skinny and dour?

Low Impedance

I stutter these things out to you

like drunk men hazard

Mingus records,

stumbling liquored over

time changes and bursts.

Like sane men let

those records jitter them

into submission—kinetic,

spat out, and it throws itself

clattering downhill. Christ.

This is me snapping

piano wires with my

fingernails, struggling

toward some unknown

lustrous chord, plunking

the bass cables and slapping at

the long spread of upper octaves.

Now at a payphone

in a stinging wind,

she calls this random corner

and, huddling in a clamshell booth,

my voice hoarses out to her,

clicking like a card on

bicycle spokes. I mutter,

I can't fight the law of averages,

and slam the receiver down,

the ringer sending

a loony note

pinging like blame

down Fulton Street,

toward Borough Hall.

Luther Missed

Once, staring into the eye of a revolver,

he cried out, swearing to a life of holiness.

The gun stuck, and the gunman shrugged.

He lived out the next twelve years in a motel

in Indiantown, watching movies on the television

inside the powder blue walls, ignoring the oath,

which followed him in the eyes of night clerks

sweeping the lobby.

True Story of the People Had Over

It was late August, in the week before

she tore off to Kansas, Colorado, and the Deep South

with my conga player—my conguero I liked

to call him, who had lent me a beautiful hat

and never asked for its return,

I don't mean this to highlight

my unburdened opinion of him, I mean

drummers are built for betrayal this

friend of mind Teresa says she fucks

them 'cause they're half the ego twice

the stamina—she called and said

she was Having People Over,

some unspecified Bon Voyage,

I remember how dumb the words sounded.

I declined. The next day when she was

gone with my conguero I drove past

Tenth Street where she lived, in this

obsessive need to spy on her roommates,

snubbing the dope vendors on their stoop.

The day they came back, I drove past

the Port Authority in the hope she and my

conguero would be happening out of the gates

and I would take them into my van, weary

and spent in each other's arms,

drive them until they fell asleep and then

abandon them at the mouth of the

Lincoln Tunnel in Hoboken. Is it Hoboken?

But no. Later when I saw her she told me

she missed me and asked if I missed her

and I said no, so she asked me again

until I lied and said yes and she won.

Miss Audrey

A man studded like a scepter on the roadside and dusted with
asphalt walks into a mansion and finds two men with money
playing ping-pong. Two men with sheet music in their bank
vaults, offices downtown near the Opera House, secretaries.
They act glad to see him but they keep playing ping-pong,
and I say, so would you like to hear him sing? And they say
yes, why don't you sing?

Nashville under low clouds, chintz everywhere and good
clean money and fun. Mansions on the edge, Homes-of-the-
Stars. Radio towers blinking; deep in their waves sings the
high lonesome sound. If a giant man came out of the Atlantic
Ocean and walked across the lower forty-eight, the city
would go like a tack into the ball of his foot. Too much blood
and beer. Everybody's too happy to look drunk. Everybody
owns an automobile. Everybody dresses like themself, back
wherever they're from they stood out like sequins on a rubber
raincoat, here everybody looks like this with big notes and
treble clefs, cacti, guitars sewn into the fabric.

* * *

And the steel guitars go: Wheeeeeee. High lonesome.

Anyhow they made him a star that afternoon. That's the kind
of men that walk around Nashville. Except it wasn't that
quick, there was some kind of papers to sign. They had to dust
him off. They bought him a song from a dumb Jew with a
piano in New York. Fake sentiment, but it's all fake in terms
of the songs, it's singers that are real. This is true whether the
song comes from someplace real or not. He sang it and these
powerful powerful men put it on vinyl and walked it over to a
radio station, and then another, and then another. It only takes
an afternoon. It only takes an afternoon.

No. That's a lie.

You want to know where the money is? I tell you. There was
a scrapyard outside of town, it was on a clay flat. They could
not put a building there because it would sink. They burrowed
into the heaps of scrap and came up with the clay. Which they
built his body out of and breathed song into. They named him
the Hillbilly Golem. That's the whole process. They didn't

have to make him a star because they acted like he was a star and nobody wanted to contradict them. They bought the records because they felt obligated, and then were seduced by it. Nobody ever got sad before that. That record ruined everything in everybody's life. Then they invented drink, and we were all hopeless.

It was the suit, not the body. You could hear the gleam on the radio. Like a halo around the sound of the record. The surface noise once the record gets real old. This was the kind of fabric that makes you want to moan out loud on the municipal bus. Blinding fabric, relentless fabric like how a lawyer makes men break down under oath. Under all the weight of all the words of their lives. It was merciless, yes. And he did regret it, yes. He never meant to hurt anybody. He said to me once, he said, Audrey, the methods of the revolution become the methods of the regime. But the killing went on. I remember the bodies that littered the streets of Nashville. We knew all of their names, once. You forgot them. I remember the charts. I remember the competition. I am the only one that remembers them now. Roy Acuff, found cut up, parts of Fred Rose spread around somebody's garden. Moon Mullican, ran through with a guitar neck. Cutesy Kitty Wells, the cunt, choked. Kill or be killed, that's the law of the hillbilly music industry.

Sometimes it seems like I'm sorry for it, now.

Outlying Seattle

Utsaladdy

Burien

Puyallup

Rosehilla

Suquamish

Portage

Issaquah

McMurray

Snoqualmie

Spanaway

Carbonado

Yelm

McKenna

Tulalip

Tumwater

Kapowsin

Tenino

Port Gamble

Monroe

Juanita

Navy Yard City

Magnolia Beach

Olalla

Lofall

Elgin

Enumclaw

Buckley

Black Diamond

Centralia

Chehalis

Steilacoom

Hadlock

Chimacum

Warm Beach

Silvana

View Park

Tukwila

Butter / Lost

Against hands, a smooth

is smoothed around

and skin

rushed up to it,

cooing sweat like a whistle

defecting a steampipe.

Oiled, the machine chuffs,

and the brain is dry, and the nerves

scurry off with messages to no one

in charge, while this equals this;

two arms locked into each other

are without a mind to differentiate

between limbs and hips, therefore,

I have come here to get lost.

The Incredible Magnetic Man

Onward to Victory, mule,

with a subatomic glimmer of rage

humming a hot inch below the cheekbones

moving down Water Street like an ox

bound in fleshy lumber, muscles and lumps

punched up and numb like insect bites

Inside the contours of veins blown up

by mosquitos into thick balloons,

a single radiowave transmits itself

into loose bits of metal scattered around;

Keys. Beltbuckles. Scissors. Headphones.

* * *

Streetlights sizzle like bees being taken to slaughter.

On Water Street, two legs

are the clack of drills

spearing into the blacktop

i n   t h e   l i g h t   f u r t h e r
d o w n

what you can only hope will be

some Imperial China is actually

the orange noise

at the ends of cigarettes

glowing at your approach

The Bug Wrangler

He was jailed for cruelty to insects, and his agent wasn't
answering the phone, so he stayed awake in the cell all
night, pictures jumping around his head of the cops and the
blowdryer they took as evidence. He used the blowdryer to
force the spiders to move, up the arm of a stuntwoman, across
a floor. He was known to the industry as a professional, that
he could coax wrenching performances from the crankiest
bugs. He was a man famed for producing bug performances
that would make people weep in the theaters.

They knew what they were jumping into, he thought, I always
split the money square, am I wrong? You take some roach
out of a miserable life and put it in pictures. Tame the wildest
insects with a flashlight and a little blowdryer technology. Go
to the beasts and teach them respect. Take them into your
home and live with them. They betray you to the police for
giving them this.

At a press conference, he sat at the microphone with a loyal
spider whom he tried to coax a positive character statement

out of, but he couldn't use the blowdryer in front of the media, and the spider stood there and said nothing while he sweated and the videotape rolled on forward.

She Got the Good Shoes, She Got the Bad Teeth

In a dim bar, the treble rose

in sharpness around her.

The frequencies went straight to the teeth.

She was meringue

in a green suit, her silver

shoes radiating,

and a shimmy that sent

her hips in a liquid

piston motion to the floor

like cream shifting in a glass.

One glance; the eye on the eye

sizzled like crayons

on super 8 film,

and she bared

angry monkey teeth at me—

each tooth its own moon

in a pollution town,

tobacco-stained pickups

on a junkstore guitar.

Bicoastal

Each city is its own dream life.

In each, the other the dream.

He is awake only on airplanes.

He hurdles weeks

through the calendar

in each city,

longing for the other.

By the Light of the Silvery Silvery

Goodnight, mud by the thousands

of whatever unit they measure mud by;

you can't move through it without missing

the angry bleached light

of usual. A bubble of humidity

forms above everything, and is

scratched open by the frictions of

machines moving

and human energies.

Hope dies and I

shake off the excess water,

spend a half hour crafting some opening

statement, but only give her my coat

and say It's a gift. For me, she says,

eyeballs floating to the top of the eye,

and I can't speak, but hand-signal: Victory.

Brecht Said Fascism Is Not the Opposite of Democracy but a Distortion of It in a Time of Crisis

A boy bought an ant farm, ants, x-ray glasses, and absolute power with nothing but proofs of purchase. He ordered them from an ad in a comic book.

He bred the ants and raised an army, and those the ants could not eat he would drive away, whimpering, by wearing the glasses and telling them in a calm but sinister voice that he could see their underwear. He conquered his own world and never had to go to sleep again. His parents came to him for mercy from the ants, but were tried and hung.

One night he collapsed after watching television without pause for two weeks. The ants, bored of destroying the lamp fixtures and wrecking the furniture, stole the glasses from his unconscious face and chased him, screaming, around the house, looking without pity upon his underwear. They ambushed him in the shower, where he hid because he felt safe behind the distorted-glass door, and ate him whole, and then were bored again.

Ketosis

That love that burns your muscles down from inside is known by the medical term Ketosis. This is the product of Anorexia. This is when the body, starved for other food, exploits other tissues for warmth. For strength. Your body consumes itself. This is where you are. You are now an onion with a spark inside it. Here I am, trying to peel each layer off, toward the essential truth in the center. Meanwhile, the center is burning outward, to reach my hand. That is, I hope it burns to meet my hand.

I do not know if you love me, or if you love your own skinniness. I love your skinniness. I love the whole of your self. I love the way you curve, and the bone under that, and whatever it is under that that moves around under my hand when my hand is on you. When my hand is on you, I can feel two things twitching—the liquid movement of your spirit from side to side, and a faint buzz, some kind of gnawing. Two loves in tandem, moving to two separate ambitions.

* * *

I do not think the love of your skinniness is the same thing as
your love for me.

This is what I do—I go to a storefront, where I buy a small
bag. The bag is made of wax paper. Inside the wax paper is a
small amount of cocaine. Then I go back to the apartment,
where you are. I pour the cocaine onto the table, and I snort
some, and sometimes you snort some. You usually don't. And
then, when that elated feeling starts to overwhelm me, my
mind is full. And then I cease to be hungry for anything,
except to fuck you, and except for my own selfish fascinations
with what is moving around in my own mind. And then I feel
like I'm actually with you.

Cocaine is interesting as a drug, because most drugs do two
things; One, they make you feel a good feeling, and B, they
make you want to have more. Cocaine is the reverse of this.
There is a good hour with cocaine, where you chatter and
jump around and a thousand things connect in your mind and
become whole and logical. But, mostly, the moment it enters
your nose you are compelled to snort more. After that hour,

the feeling becomes incidental. The feeling is a side effect in a blur of consumption for its own sake.

In that hour, we fuck on the couch, and then we fuck in the bed. And after, both gaunt bodies stay locked, trembling a little from the shock of release and all the burning going on inside them. And then, locked to you, I start to babble and babble. Something about the drug allows me to talk without caring if you hear me or not. Because you look absorbed. You're elsewhere. Every part of you is concentrated on some inner point where you're choosing some muscle to burn, some nerve to throw on the fire. Every part of your conscious mind is tracing the inside shell of the onion, looking for specks of fuel. My body unlocks and begins to search the outside world for more.

So I leave, and when I'm at the door, I say; Do you want anything? And you say; No. Nothing. And I say; Are you sure. And you say; No. Nothing.

And I go, and then I'm back, with more. You're on the same couch. You're still naked, maybe with a shirt thrown loose on your skinny shoulders, or a blanket wrapped around the grill of your ribs. Your eyes are still focused somewhere else. Maybe you do a little, and the spark in the onion eases up on the inner layers and burns the cocaine for a while. Or maybe you smoke a cigarette, and the spark laps at the fumes. But your body becomes exhausted, and you fall asleep, askew on the cushions.

I am awake for hours, spastic, walking around the room, one eye watching you sleep. You don't look like you're dreaming at all. When I lay down, I try not to move. Though everything about me is astutter, I try not to startle you awake. I sleep, eventually.

In the morning, I make coffee before you're awake. I am for some reason compelled to stumble out of the bed at an insanely early hour, my head stuck up with thickness, my muscles slack and useless. When you rise, we drink the coffee, yours with milk. My body consoles itself with the minor stimulant. And, in yours, somewhere in the center, the spark licks at the trickle of nourishment.

Bedspins

Drunk, she was carried

and thrown into the pillows.

She stamped her foot on the floor

as she slept, to keep the world

from spinning away from her

like a troubled childhood.

Descent of Tools

Iron chunks fight upward

to the surface of the world;

The simple ax

was made to make

the candlestick

was made to make

the blunderbuss

was made to make

the lock, moveable type

was made to make

the steam engine

was made to make

the outboard motor, the toaster, the transistor,

was made to make

the speaker that sings to you

while we speak, now.

Your only instinct is convenience,

and the hand of your convenience

moves to build a mind

superior to yours.

Long Gone from Vaudeville

The infamous comedian in

business class pauses

lips over plastic;

the liquid whooshes down

with pills between tight

nervous breaths; he lets

the throat relax; sleep.

Four hours pass.

At the carousel in a stupor,

pawing through autographs.

The Boy Is a Fraud

You can be

anything

as long

as you got

the shoes

to prove it;

as long as you got

the walk down;

as long as you don't

flinch

This can be

all you

for real

you can go

all these places

for real

You can say

this belongs to you

for real

you can clutch

your reference books

and conjure

the fine words out

with your fine thin fingers

small and

circling above

the pages

stirring up

allies

in your defense

against language

as a thing

which is

not pretty

but actually

speaks.

You want proof

that you are

what the shoes

connote;

not clean thoughts

but lush music

and you

lie awake

sweating

wondering where you

bought the myth

wondering how much

it costs

to make your pain

valid.

Whose Music?

He lives in absolute terror of a saxophone he has kept under his bed for four years. He played it since his mouth learned to blow, then put it under the bed four years ago because he had grown bored of it and moved on to affairs with lovelier instruments; a clarinet for two months, a flute for awhile, the drums. He went back to the saxophone and couldn't face it unashamed, so he put it under the bed and learned to play sociology, the jewel of all musical instruments. This all had something to do with the difference between fingerpainting and Jackson Pollock, or Motherwell, or when a man plays stupid noise he finds attractive on a violin he can't play, as opposed to the man who can play études but chooses to screech. The joy, the redemptive power of the horn he felt unentitled to, as if he had to pay more to get his interest back from the saxophone.

Now he fears the saxophone will end up in his mouth like a crackpipe, that twenty years from now he will look back on that one delirious hour with the reed in his mouth, his fingers tapping the brass, and regret it forever. That he will end up some sham Anthony Braxton, always in fear that people will discover him as a fraud. Or that he would spend the rest of his life like Anthony Braxton, scribbling pictures of bicycles and numbers to describe tunes that, language having been stolen from him by the music, he can't name.

Yesterday he remembered his affair with the clarinet, momentarily on the D train, over the Manhattan Bridge, and was momentarily swept upward by the memory of the clarinet's wood smell. This somehow coupled with the scenery, the blue riveted-iron bridge that colored his memory like a drink mixed with mathematics and Duke Ellington.

Here's How It Ends

Here's how it ends: he gets the girl. He gets the money. His
loyal sidekick jumps up from behind the rock and shouts Hey!
distracting the firing squad. The sidekick is cut down, but
the girl and he escape through the treacherous badlands, and
the sidekick ascends to Glory in an orchestra of sentiment.
Around the vicious curve, his car skids by sideways, on two
wheels, while the enemy careens over a cliff and is tumbling,
tumbling, tumbling, and explodes! In a fight, he knocks the
enemy off the scaffolding and leaps into the water before the
gas tank explodes! He parachutes into the green mountains
before the smoking plane explodes! She fears him drowned,
but he emerges from the sea! The mysterious sheik removes
his veil and is not the sheik at all, but the sidekick, not dead!
The sidekick is not dead at all! The girl is not dead at all!
The palace is on fire but the king alive! The oil tanker is sunk
but the lovable captain alive! The rocket is wrecked but the
robot walks! The Cadillac is swallowed by the quicksand,
but the happy pimp with the heart of gold laughs, though

the briefcase full of money sinks with it, in the trunk! Why?
Because the money is counterfeit!

The detective slays the monster! The explorer defeats the mad
scientist! The boy defeats the alien! The average man conquers
the forces of darkness! And then he is with the girl.

And then he is with the girl.
And then he is with the girl.
And then he receives his rich reward.
And then he kisses the girl.
And then the sun goes down.
In the life raft.
On the shore.
In the plucky little town.
On the frozen tundra.
In the speeding convertible.
In the posh watering holes of Glittering Manhattan.
In the lush jungle.
On the dock.
In glamorous Monte Carlo.
In mysterious old Baghdad.
In the desert.

In the forest.

In the hills.

On the courthouse steps.

In the center of the sea.

Transatlantic

Only sex and flight lost time like this.

Pop songs are curves of the same length,

outside the sight of the clock.

In this plane,

above this ocean,

my headphones swell with

bitter melodies

candied in echoplex

and fattened violins,

cooed at by low thrums

that reshape themselves

into your open mouth,

your hips slithering around me.

There is a tiny gap in my mind,

where the moan you made sat.

I only remember how it felt to hear it.

It comes back to me like a song I heard and loved,

but that dissipated, leaving

a phantom trace of notes in sequence

that probably doesn't exist. I can hear

the breath around it, though,

and as the plane jitters through turbulence,

as the melody, cupped to the sides of my head

like your hands did slants

toward a lush and glorious crash

of cymbals and chords, your tongue stirs

a weird magic into the mix.

Outside the window of the plane,

there is nothing,

and under that,

water and water and water.

Printed in the United States
by Baker & Taylor Publisher Services